"When I pray, I don't always get what I want, but I get what I need. In vocal prayer we go to God on foot. In meditation, we go to God on horseback. In contemplation we go to God in a jet."

~ Venerable Fulton Sheen

A New Hope

God in the Time of COVID-19

Book II

Further reflections for difficult times

Edited by Matthew Betts

The National Shrine of

ST. JUDE

Faversham, Kent

www.stjudeshrine.org.uk

First published by the Shrine of Saint Jude (Carmelite Charitable Trust) on 16 July 2021 - Feast of Our Lady of Mount Carmel

Shrine of Saint Jude, Carmelite Friars, PO Box 289, FAVERSHAM, Kent, ME13 3BZ
www.stjudeshrine.org.uk

ISBN 13 (print edition) **978-0-904849-60-8**

Edited and designed by Mr Matthew Betts

Front cover designed by Miss Kerry Betts, The Happy Tea Company; Photo taken by Mr Matthew Betts at Whitstable, Kent

Printed in the United Kingdom

Dedicated to the memory of Father Kevin Alban, O.Carm (1958 - 2021)

This book is also for all the children of the world: true heroes of the Pandemic - particularly, Adam, Abigail, Alex, Analena, Ciara, Clara, Daniel, Dhalia, Ellie, Elliot, Esther, Gabriel, Hannah, Isabelle B, Isabelle OB, James, Jessica B, Jessica H, Joseph, Joshua, Lilia, Martha, Megan, Millie, Niamh, Naomi, Olivia, Ophelia, Orla, Phoebe, Rafe, Raphael, Rosabella, Sophie, Thérèse, Thomas, Tom, William and Zach.

Thank you to Claudine, Stephen, David, Judy, Nimal, Tracey, Matthew, Ella, James and Emily for being lockdown Zoom friends, as well as friends for life.

Dedicated to the memory of
Father Kevin Alban, O.Carm
(1958 - 2021)

CONTENTS

FOREWORD

Fr Brendan Grady, O.Carm

As we each do our best to continue living with the effects of the COVID-19 pandemic, there seems to be, among many, a renewed appreciation of our need for one another. Human beings form and are shaped by compassionate, caring communities. Much effort is still needed to sustain our sense of balance, rhythm, inner joy and hope. As friends of Saint Jude - our patron saint of hope - we live with an awareness of a loving God who is passionate about our wellbeing and will never desert us.

We have experienced restrictions, disturbance, dismay, disillusionment, isolation and powerlessness during an international crisis that brought our world to its knees, but we can take courage in knowing that eventually it will pass. If we find ourselves lacking motivation, we know we are not alone and can only do our best to be faithful to what matters most.

The reflections you are about to read were originally published online. We are pleased that they are now available in this second book of reflections since the onslaught of the pandemic in 2020. We hope that they will help you in some way now and in the future during the difficult times you may experience.

The book has been dedicated to the memory of our Carmelite brother, Father Kevin Alban, O.Carm, who died on 4 May 2021. We thank all who have shared their reflections and the Most Rev. John Wilson, Archbishop of Southwark, who has written the Afterword.

The great Carmelite mystic, Saint Teresa of Avila said:

"Let nothing disturb you. Let nothing frighten you. All things pass: God never changes. Patience obtains all things. Whoever has God lacks nothing. God alone suffices."

As we move forward towards a new horizon beyond COVID-19, our Carmelite communities in Britain continue to hold you in our hearts when we pray. Together we allow our faith to be reignited, our sense of being disciples of Jesus to be deepened, and our expressions of practical love to be filled with commitment and joy.

INTRODUCTION

Mr Matthew Betts

"Humble yourselves before the Lord, and he will lift you up" - James 4:10

Back in 2020, Fr Kevin Alban wrote to the friends of Saint Jude in our quarterly newsletter 'Carmelite News' about how we were trying to avoid alienating those who do not have computers or the internet. In this Pandemic, we need to avoid this new divide.

Thus, at the Shrine of Saint Jude, we continued to produce our printed newsletter and the normal novenas and shared masses associated with it. We also re-directed the Shrine Office phone to my home so I could continue to answer queries whilst the rest of the team split their time at home and the office. In addition, we published many of the online reflections from 2020 in the book 'God in the Time of COVID-19'.

Unfortunately, the resolution of this Pandemic crisis took longer than anyone anticipated and so I decided to reintroduce the online reflections, but on a weekly basis. We also introduced another theme of reflection: 'Pandemic Heroes'. I am pleased that we have been able to put together another edition of reflections that cover 2021 and some from 2020. This book is about the 'Pandemic Heroes' and the new hope as we perhaps move out of these difficult times.

In these already tough times of 2021, Father Kevin Alban, O.Carm died after a short illness, aged 62 years. Father Kevin had accepted what was happening with great peace. He said, *"Very few people have the grace of knowing that they are going to die soon."* We are very grateful to him for all his support of these online reflections and this book is dedicated to his memory. May he Rest in Peace and rise in glory!

I would like to thank each of the writers who were not only kind enough to write for the series of reflections, but have also allowed us to print them again in this book. Thank you also to the proof readers (Alex, Derek, Marcus) for checking this book so thoroughly - though any mistakes are mine. It hasn't been possible to include all of the online reflections in this booklet, but I hope that I have been able to pick a varied selection.

Finally, I would like to thank Terri and our children for always being understanding throughout my work, especially whilst I put together this book. Thank you too to the Shrine Office team, Fr Brendan Grady and to the management group for continued support.

CONTRIBUTORS

Kevin Alban, O.Carm was a Carmelite friar of the British Province. He was Prior Provincial for the Order in Britain. Kevin previously served as General Secretary and General Bursar in Rome. He died in 2021.

Sister Benedict OSB is a Benedictine Nun of Saint Mildred's Priory, Minster Abbey, Kent.

Johan Bergström-Allen, TOC is a lay member of the Carmelite Order and worked as the Communications and Outreach Manager for the Carmelites.

Matthew Betts is the lay development manager and data lead for the Shrine and Trust. He is married with two children.

Veronica Errington is married and lives in West Lancashire. She is a member of the Third Order of Carmel, and is currently its national secretary.

Tim Finigan is a parish priest of the Archdiocese of Southwark.

Nicole Gallop Mildon is a Guild of Saint Jude Life member and a supporter of the Shrine. She is a lawyer based in London and volunteers in Lourdes for two weeks each year.

Brendan Grady, O.Carm is a Carmelite friar in the British Province. He is currently parish priest at the Church of Our Lady of Mount Carmel, chaplain of the Shrine of Saint Jude, and Administrator of the British Province.

Francis Kemsley, O.Carm is a Carmelite friar in the British Province. He is currently Prior of Aylesford, but previously he was Shrine Director at the Shrine of Saint Jude.

Nicholas King, SJ is a Jesuit priest who is currently Assistant Catholic Chaplain at Oxford University. He has recently published a translation of the entire Greek Bible.

CONTRIBUTORS

Paul de Groot, O.Carm is a Carmelite friar in the British Province. He is a member of the Carmelite community in Aylesford.

Andy Joyce is a Guild of Saint Jude Life member and has been a supporter of the Shrine for many years. He is a teacher based in Bradford and volunteers in Lourdes for two weeks each year.

Aldrick Monteiro was originally from Pakistan, coming to England in 1960 as a young boy. In 1972 he was diagnosed with schizophrenia which he has been fighting ever since.

Trish Murphy is a parishioner at Our Lady of Mount Carmel in Faversham, and a regular volunteer and Guild member of the Shrine of Saint Jude.

Hugh Parry is a Permanent Deacon in Portsmouth Diocese. He is married with five children and many grandchildren.

Colette Sharrock is a Guild of Saint Jude Life member and has been a supporter of the Shrine for a while. She lives near Cambridge and volunteers in Lourdes for two weeks each year.

Peter Tyler is Professor of Pastoral Theology and Spirituality in London.

Gerard Walsh, O.Carm is a Carmelite friar in the British Province. He is part of the Carmelite community in Aylesford and works with the youth in Southwark.

Archbishop John Wilson was appointed Archbishop of Southwark by Pope Francis on 10 June 2019. His Installation took place in Saint George's Cathedral, Southwark, on the Feast of St James the Apostle.

If the soul is seeking God,
so much more is God seeking the soul.
~ Saint John of the Cross

Pandemic Heroes

FOR THE BINMEN (WASTE DISPOSAL OPERATIVES)

Br Paul de Groot, O.Carm

The virus and the first lockdown gave us a realisation of how dependant we are on each other and especially on "key" workers.
We have clapped for some like those in the NHS and carers.
We have seen and appreciated those in the supermarkets,
or those who deliver our post or online parcels.
But I'm in awe of those unsung heroes the binmen.

They have to visit every household with no idea where that virus may be lurking.
They have to work together in a cab where they cannot keep socially distant.
They have worked through the heat of the summer (with festering bins),
the torrential autumn rains and now through ice and cold.

Because we have stayed at home, their workload has increased.
but the time to do the job has not.
And, as their colleagues have had to isolate or succumbed, who can "volunteer" to plug the gap?

However hard they strive how angry do we get if our bins are not emptied on time?

And where is the social justice for our key workers?
As the first lockdown ended there was no sign of a fundamental change in our attitude to how we value and appreciate key workers,
not even by paying them what we think they are really worth.

It seems we want to see no change.
The wealthy who do not need to work for a salary have got wealthier.
Those who do need a wage are having to struggle more and more
despite all the help the government gives.
How many key workers have to resort to food banks
(a scandal for us all that they have to exist)?

Let us pray....

Loving and gracious God,
Pour blessings on those who collect our waste.
Encourage and strengthen them in their work.
Keep them safe from all harm.
Stir up within us a hunger to ensure they and all key workers are fairly paid and treated; we ask this through Christ our Lord. Amen.

Reflection was first published online on 30 April 2021

CAPTAIN TOM

Matthew Betts

In many ways, Captain Tom showed us all how important it is to love your neighbour, especially during the tough times of a Pandemic. He became a hero to many of us - indeed, a Pandemic Hero.

Captain Sir Tom, who was given the honorary title of colonel on his 100th birthday, had initially set out to raise £1,000 for NHS charities by walking laps of the 82ft (25m) loop in his garden in Marston Moretaine, Bedfordshire. But he eventually raised £32,794,701 from more than one and a half million supporters.

May the souls of all the faithful departed, through the mercy of God, rest in peace. Here at the Shrine and across the country, the Carmelites continue to pray for all those affected by this Pandemic. May Captain Tom rest in peace and rise in glory!

Jesus answered, "Love the Lord your God with all your heart, with all your soul, and with all your mind." This is the greatest and the most important commandment. The second most important commandment is like it: "Love your neighbour as you love yourself." Captain Tom did exactly that.

Reflection was first published online on 2 February 2021

CARING FOR OTHERS

Mrs Colette Sharrock

When I retired from Addenbrookes hospital in Cambridge I decided that I still had enough energy to continue working and chose to become a carer in the Community. Many of the people I cared for were living alone and usually lonely. I was possibly the only person they saw and spoke with each day. Apart from the routine of washing and dressing and preparing their food I tried to make time to chat. They loved to tell their life stories and they loved to reminisce. Some didn't have families nearby; some did have families, but sadly never saw them very much.

This, of course, was long before the Pandemic and now there are many more people feeling alone and isolated. However, throughout these difficult times, carers have continued their work.

We can't all be carers, but with a little effort we could all make a difference by making a call to someone we know is alone just to say hello; how are you? It would mean so much to them.

Why don't you do that today?

Let us pray...

Lord, give us the wisdom to know ourselves, the humility to accept ourselves as we really are and the courage and independence to defend what we know to be right. Help us to respect the needs of others, being always ready to dedicate our own talents to their service.

Give us the strength to suffer the trials and tensions of life with fortitude and the vision to see through suffering to the peace which lies beyond.

May we by our tolerance be a constant support to each other and a source of strength to our families whom we commend to Your care.

Reflection was first published online on 9 April 2021

COVID-19 TESTS

Mrs Nicole Gallop Mildon

Since October 2020 I have had many COVID-19 tests, not because I have been exposed, but to enable me to visit my mother in a nursing home, who has been granted in person visits on medical grounds.

Three days before each visit, I have a PCR test, and at first the results took 2.5 to 3 days to arrive. But the results have been coming faster and faster, the latest took just 14 hours and the result arrived in an email at 3 a.m.

It reminded me that the Covid testing regime functions 24/7 including during public holidays. I know tests were being processed over the Christmas weekend, with the same speed as normal. The staff in all the labs are working around the clock, tirelessly, handling samples, most of which have come from someone who has symptoms.

We do not know their names, or faces, but they work away quietly behind the scenes making an enormous and unsung contribution to the fight against Covid. Theirs is a hidden front line.

The work of those in the labs reminds me of Chapter 6 of Matthew's Gospel, where we are instructed to *"go to your inner room, close the door, and pray to your Father in secret*", for the staff are working hidden behind the closed doors of their labs. The whole of the chapter is worth reading for it teaches us about the three pillars of Lent: prayer, almsgiving and fasting as well as giving us the words of the Lord's Prayer.

It closes with a prayer that is well worth repeating in these strange times: *"Do not worry about tomorrow; tomorrow will take care of itself. Sufficient for a day is its own evil."*

Let us pray...

Lord, we give thanks for all who work in the testing laboratories in hidden service to their fellow man. As we wait for an end to this pandemic, we reflect on the instruction not to worry about tomorrow, but trust in you, our Heavenly Father. Amen

Reflection was first published online on 16 April 2021

CHILDREN

Mr Matthew Betts

"I have no greater joy than to hear that my children are walking in the truth."

- 3 John 1:4

One Pandemic Hero that we have not written about yet is the children. Children have faced so much because of lockdown and more, such as schools closing and not being able to enjoy social interactions with people outside their family for weeks on end. I am writing this as a dad to two primary school age children. Their mum has been working as a nurse in A&E throughout the Pandemic, and I have been working from home as Development Manager and data lead. During the two lockdowns – like many other parents – when my wife was home, she would home-school; and when she was not, I would home-school.

As parents, we work hard to protect and nurture our children through our actions and beliefs. In the early days of this Pandemic, there was a lot of fear about the unknown – what is this disease; how do you catch it; what are we going to do; how are we going to teach our children; will there be enough food and toilet paper; is it safe to go to the shops? Meanwhile, the children were steadily becoming aware that something very serious and wrong was coming along, but they trusted their parents wholeheartedly. We therefore tried to keep conversations about this Pandemic away from their earshot and watch the news once they were in bed (not always possible).

Adults should be particularly proud of how resilient we have all been at following the rules and keeping safe. However, it is the children who have come along with us that have remained the strongest – due, I think, to that trust in their parents and other adults.

When you really dig deep, it is quite heart-breaking to realise what the Pandemic has given to our children: fear; closed schools (at first a novelty and then a bit boring); no birthday parties since March 2020 (an important part of making friends and making greater friends – my daughter hasn't been to any in her first year at school); no 'sleepovers'; no visits to Father Christmas or Christmas fairs; no proper holiday (just a stay-cation); no visits to older relatives (such an important connection); no visits to uncles, aunts, grandparents or hugs from them; no nativity play; no visits to theatres, cinemas or art galleries; and more.

And then, unfortunately, many children have also experienced the death of relatives or friends who always feel so far away because we cannot see anyone. We have lost relatives and friends during the Pandemic – none of them because of COVID-19 - but that does not make it any easier.

This Pandemic makes the 'normal' grieving process very difficult.

However, throughout all of this our children have remained stoic and resilient: what amazing heroes they are. Like many parents, it was a relief when the children could return to school – and what a change in them once they were back. School is really the best place for our children (though I did enjoy teaching them the names of all the kings and queens of England and how to play chess!).

"Rejoice always, pray without ceasing, give thanks in all circumstances; for this is the will of God in Christ Jesus for you." - 1 Thessalonians 5:16-18

Throughout the Pandemic, the children have provided hope. We are therefore reminded about the events after Jesus's death: the apostles and disciples had gone through so much pain and had lost their friend and leader, Jesus. They were scared and had locked themselves away, so the authorities could not find them. However, then Jesus came to see them after his death and Resurrection, and said, "Peace be with you." From then on, they were filled with the hope that the Risen Christ brings.

As Pope Francis said in 2019: *"Each of us is called…to rediscover in the Risen Christ the one who rolls back from our heart the heaviest of stones…Do not fear, then: the Lord loves your life, even when you are afraid to look at it and take it in hand… Jesus is a specialist at turning our deaths into life… Easter teaches us that believers do not linger at graveyards, for they are called to go forth to meet the Living One."*

Therefore the children have been our hope and their resilience has been our hope. My son said to me a few weeks ago, *"things will get better, daddy – don't you worry"*. He is right. Let us make sure this world is fit for the children and a good place to live. Thank you children - our true Pandemic Heroes.

Let us pray…

Father, whose Son called children to him,
we pray for boys and girls everywhere,
that these children may
be filled with laughter and happiness.
As they learn so many facts
and enter into so many new experiences,
may they learn of your love,
and how to serve Jesus as Master and Lord. (Bernard Thorogood, 1927 – 2020)

Reflection was first published online on 7 May 2021

FUNERAL DIRECTORS

Deacon Hugh Parry

Rightly, we have been remembering our front-line workers throughout the pandemic. Firstly, and rightly, we have remembered those in the health service who have often put their own lives and those of their families at risk to care for us all. Add to that the members of the other emergency services, retail workers in essential goods, teachers and so on. The list seems endless which is good because, if nothing else, it reminds us how much we rely on each other all the time. This is important because there is a disturbing tendency to believe we lead independent lives, when we are always heavily dependent on so many others.

When thinking of those ministries we rely on and turn to in times of stress, how many of you have considered Undertakers or Funeral Directors as one such ministry? In the two parishes I serve in my diaconal ministry, we are praying each week for all those providing this essential service. One local funeral director I know well personally, caught COVID-19 and has only just returned to work. Another small family firm has twenty-two funerals in the process of being arranged and they said to us that they feel overlooked.

This is incredibly sad when it is considered that they offer a 24/7 service and I know of some whom are working 18-hour days six or seven days a week. At funerals, I make a point of asking how they are and how they are coping. The fact that I bother to ask, and their returned gratitude is testament to the fact that they do feel overlooked and unappreciated. I wonder if our personal reluctance to ask them is because we realise that at some point, we will all need their services.

Let us remember that Joseph of Arimathea and Nicodemus brought linen and a mixture of myrrh and aloes, in which to wrap the body of Jesus. Just quietly, they efficiently did what had to be done while others were grieving.

Let us pray for those who serve us in our grief:

Lord you entered fully into our suffering through the cross of Christ Jesus, proclaiming that there is nowhere, not even death, that can escape your eternal love for us. Into the pain and reality of death, you raise up people to care for our mortal bodies. They prepare us for our goodbyes and accompany the dead to their burial. We pray for all who delicately and compassionately labour at the time of death. Bless and keep your servants safe, give them strength as they bear witness to your holy presence among us. Amen.

Reflection was first published online on 19 February 2021

FRONTLINE WORKERS

Sister Benedict, OSB

During the pandemic, I have been reflecting on the lives of our Pandemic Heroes and I am praying today especially for one of them, let's call him Luke: As a frontline worker in a hospital, Luke is risking his life daily to help others who are suffering as a result of another illness, just as potentially deadly as COVID-19.

I marvel at his kind, generous, warm and outgoing nature. One day in conversation about the intercession of Saints to heal, knowing that I was a Catholic, he shared the following with me:

'As a young child I was very withdrawn and so was very difficult for my mother to cope with. Although our background was Hindu, my mother used to visit a Catholic Church. A statue of Saint Jude was in a little niche there. On discovering that he was known as the 'Patron Saint for hopeless cases' she decided to bring me to this shrine. She lifted up my little body to touch the statue and from then on, my personality changed dramatically. As you can see! So I believe in miracles.'

Saint Jude had never been part of my life until that day. I pray that this Saint will help us to come through these difficult days with a renewed faith and greater love for the whole of creation.

I think of the words of the song by Lennon and McCartney: *'Hey Jude, take a sad song and make it better...'*

Let us pray to him for all frontline workers:

Merciful Lord through the intercession of St Jude,
Be with all frontline workers and those they care for.
Be with their families and loved ones.
We pray especially for those who feel that their situation is hopeless.
With you there is always hope.
Your mercy never fails and your compassion is without bounds
We make our prayer though Christ our Lord. Amen.

Reflection was first published online on 21 May 2021

THE HIDDEN CARERS

Mrs Maggie Cascioli

When John was five he went almost every evening to the local shop and, with considerable skill, took bread, butter, crisps...He occasionally stole cold meats but very rarely sweets. The elderly shop owner, intrigued by what John stole, began to watch him carefully. Gradually he realised that John was hungry, that he never stole anything which needed opening or cooking. The owner also thought that, given the amount stolen, John was probably stealing food for others as well as for himself.

When the shop owner eventually contacted Social Services, they discovered that John and his two younger siblings lived with their grandmother. She was not deliberately unkind but she was an alcoholic so after buying her essentials there was very little left for necessities like food.

There are, I suspect, many children, people like John who quietly take on the care of others.

There have always been 'hidden' carers, many of them family members, sometimes children: teenagers who long before 'lock down' delivered papers but who now deliver shopping to their neighbours; the shop assistant who puts aside milk and the paper for an elderly customer; the woman who 'gossips' through the window with her shielding neighbour; the mother who schools her children, cooks, cleans and still 'works from home'...

Let us pray...

We pray for all those who, like Saint Joseph, care for others quietly and unobtrusively...
For those who put their own needs after those of others...
For those whose actions and words oil the wheels of our society
For all those who are unobtrusively kind
May they find the energy to continue to do this
Pour out on them your grace and peace
We ask this through Christ our Lord... Amen.

Reflection was first published online on 23 April 2021

NURSES

Mr Matthew Betts

Here we are again in what a lot of people are calling 'Lockdown 3.0'. My wife is an A&E nurse - it's a tough environment to work in at the moment - so we can feel proud that we are all doing something to help with the greater good and to stop the virus spreading.

I just wanted to reflect on my wife's day when she goes to A&E, so you know that everyone working in there is a hero. Terri is a mother of two children, so she wakes up and helps me out with breakfast before she heads out. The children have never really understood (nor would we want them to) the dangers of her going to work at the moment.

My wife is trained as a paediatric nurse, but she also has skills and knowledge to look after adults, especially useful at the moment because fewer children are coming to A&E so she is required to work with the surge in Covid-positive adults. She works a mixture of shifts ranging from eight to thirteen hours. A&E is currently (January 2021) very busy and she has to wear PPE at all times. It's also very hot, and it can be difficult to even have a sip of water or pop to the toilet between designated break times.

COVID-19 isn't interested in ages. My wife has looked after critically ill patients from the ages of 20 to 99 with horrible symptoms of the disease, many of whom were previously fit and well - which can be distressing for staff to witness. This is made more difficult by visitors not being allowed to stay with patients.

At the end of a very hot and gruelling day, Terri will get out of her PPE and say a little prayer to God, "please Lord look after everyone here today". She will then get changed, head home, but not get close to her family until she has had a hot shower. The children, of course, have been home all day and are itching to see their mummy (they are bored of daddy!), but have to be a bit more patient.

As we are in lockdown, I will then go up to work to catch up, so after that hard work at A&E, my wife has to "take over" children duties and look after them. By February, this doesn't work so well because we are all exhausted and never see each other - so I start to work a few hours on Saturday to catch up. Throughout all of this, Terri remains unflappable and has a constant smile and calming presence - at home and away. Amazing.

Nurses, doctors, porters, cleaners, receptionists, and everyone else are truly amazing and they deserve so much praise. Thank you God.

Reflection was first published online on 8 January 2021

PARAMEDICS

Mrs Veronica Errington

Even in 'normal' times paramedics launch themselves into the most demanding situations. They are not so much the healers of the medical profession, but the rescuers. They arrive to the sound of sirens, working under conditions of stress with the need to make split-second decisions by which a life can be saved – or lost; whether on a busy motorway, a city street, or the quiet domestic midnight scene, their work is accompanied by panic and grief.

Pope Francis once described the Church of our times as a field hospital. This image has become more vivid to me as a result of the pandemic and the role of those who serve on the very front of that front line. Paramedics are masters of damage limitation; they deal with the immediate need and entrust the process of healing to others.

We are in the grip of an emergency. For many, there has been no time to properly mourn the death of a friend or family member. Perhaps Macbeth's words on the death of his wife resonate:

"She should have died hereafter/There would have been a time for such a word."

Thank God for paramedics! They work on the edge of what is possible, risking their own lives and risking failure in order to save whomsoever they can. They also point to something beyond: Jesus, the supreme paramedic, who raised Jairus' daughter, and restored a son to the widow of Nain. They point to the powerful help of saints such as Saint Jude, that helper in time of failing hope.

Paramedics also remind me of two things about my faith: I am both in need of spiritual first aid and at the same time called to help others. On the one hand, I can pray the words of the Anima Christi:

"Blood of Christ fill all my veins/ Water from Christ's side wash out my stains."

And yet, at the same time, acting out of that same 'sickness', I can try and reach out to those in my path, using the comfort we have received to comfort others.

Reflection was first published online on 5 March 2021

POLITICIANS

Fr Nicholas King, SJ

As the effects of our pandemic have been unfolding, there are many groups of people whom we have come to see differently as we watch what is going on: nurses and cleaners and teachers are obvious examples. But what about that favourite target of all our derision, the politicians? Now put down that rotten tomato; this is not the time to be throwing fruit at other people, no matter how unpopular.

Politicians, you see, are not 'in it just for what they can get out of it'; for the most part they are where they are because they wanted to serve their country, assisted, no doubt, by a healthy dose of the ambition that helped them get there. You must give them some credit for having tried to deal with the Coronavirus when, a little over a year ago, we had hardly heard the word; the manual of instructions had not yet been written, and what seems obvious to us now as observers of the scene, must at the beginning have seemed to them very far from self-evident.

You might think of Pontius Pilate, perhaps; he simply cannot work out who Jesus is, or how to handle him. Look at John's Gospel (18:33-35); Pilate is a politician whose job absolutely depends on keeping the peace, at a very sensitive time of the year, and dealing with people he hardly understood (Jewish nationalism was always very heated at Passover, it being the celebration of God's having liberated Israel from oppression in Egypt). You can also feel that he wants to go deeper into the mystery of Jesus: *"Are you the King of the Jews?...What have you done?", he asks.* And Jesus' response, it must be said, does not offer much help: *"My Kingdom is not of this world"*. At the end, all Pilate can do in response to Jesus' reference to "*everyone who is of the truth*" is to ask, "*What is Truth?*", a profoundly philosophical question, which does not get the debate much further forward. Would it be a good idea for you, this week, to pray for politicians, especially those you most dislike? They have a very difficult task.

Let us pray...

God of power and might, wisdom and justice,
through you authority is rightly administered,
laws are enacted, and judgment is decreed.
May they always seek the ways of righteousness, justice and mercy.
Grant that they may be enabled by your powerful protection
to lead our country with honesty and integrity.
We ask this through Christ our Lord. Amen.

Reflection was first published online on 12 March 2021

POSTAL WORKERS

Fr Gerard Walsh, O.Carm

I was very interested and pleased to learn that Gabriel the Archangel is the Patron Saint of Postal Workers. I thought that they could have no greater saint as their patron. Gabriel was God's messenger who brought news of great joy to Mary at the Annunciation, to Zechariah in the temple, concerning the birth of John the Baptist, to Joseph in a dream, telling him to take Mary as his wife and then to the Shepherds in the fields at the Birth of Jesus.

During this time of Pandemic, our Postal Workers have continued to brave the virus as well as all weathers and difficult situations, to bring important news, greetings and communications to our communities, especially the elderly and isolated who may not have access to the internet and email.

Probably one of the worst parts of the lockdown has been the isolation so many of our older and infirm people have experienced – parents and grandparents not being able to meet with their children and grandchildren. The Postal Service has provided the means for that all-important contact. Their service has been and continues to be invaluable to all our communities, especially allowing us to keep in touch by means of greetings cards and letters. The Postal Workers deserve our deep appreciation, working in what can only be described as very trying circumstances.

I would like to highlight the dedicated service of all Postal Workers both at home and abroad. We commend them to your prayers and we say a great big THANK YOU!

Let us pray...

Loving and gracious God,
we ask you to bless all Postal Workers.
Keep them in your special care,
and keep them safe as they continue to carry out their duties,
especially during this time of Pandemic and Lockdown.
We ask this through Christ our Lord.
AMEN

Reflection was first published online on 29 January 2021

TEACHERS

Mr Andy Joyce

As I sit at home looking through my window at the snow, I could never have envisaged that I would be preparing and teaching online lessons to my students again in less than twelve months. Strangely, it reminds me of the lady who hit the headlines in 2019 at the start of the General Election campaign with, "What another one!", but here we are for the third time in lockdown.

Again, our routines have been disrupted, and we have had to change how we interact with each other. Under normal circumstances, I am constantly used to "Sir, Sir", being shouted in my ear, but now all is quiet, and I get an email instead. It's not really the same, but my students still need help. Of course, we all need help from time to time, and just as I try to guide my students online, we teachers too have needed help, be it emotional, physical, or virtual.

What has struck me this time is that the little things I can do will go a long way to help someone. One of my students, whom I have not seen for several weeks, joined one of my online classes. I asked her why it had taken her so long to join the class after so long. Her reply was that she was doing all her work and was getting on with it, but recently the one thing she missed most of all was seeing a face from school. In 'normal' times, we take this for granted, and never give it a thought, but now we crave to see people face to face (without a mask), and I wonder how we will all react once this pandemic is over. I for one, look forward to the day when I can see my students face to face, and see their expressions on their faces.

Seeing people face to face reminded me of Saint Thérèse of Lisieux, and her love for the Holy Face of Jesus. In her book 'Story of a Soul', she contemplates Jesus's Holy Face, which is the star that guides her steps. Let our faces guide those lonely faces during this pandemic, so that we may all see each other in the face of Jesus.

Let us pray...

Jesus! Thy dear and holy Face
Is the bright star that guides my way;
Thy gentle glance, so full of grace,
Is my true heaven on earth, today.
My love finds out the holy charm
Of Thy dear eyes with tear-drops wet;
Through mine own tears I smile at Thee,
And in Thy griefs my pains forget. Amen.

Reflection was first published online on 12 February 2021

THESE ARE THE HANDS

Fr Francis Kemsley, O.Carm

I thought that 2020 would be remembered for Brexit but how wrong I was as it was dominated by news of COVID-19. As a Carmelite I have reflected upon Mary. She treasured in her heart what was asked of her. She stood silently at the foot of the cross. Her presence is an inspiration for all mothers and others who have suffered the loss of their loved one. The intercession of Mary has long been sought in times of sickness and plague. Many of you will be aware that the Shrine of Our Lady of Rue du Bac and thus, the devotion of the Miraculous Medal had its origins in Paris during the plague of 1830.

The Shrine of Saint Jude is still closed (February 2021), and many of you have not been able to attend mass or go to your local church. Despite self-isolation and social distancing, we have discovered new and creative ways of 'being together' and becoming the Body of Christ while complying with Government and Church directives. Though, there is great pain at not being able to celebrate publicly the sacraments. It is good that we can be together each week virtually, but I also know many of the friends of the Carmelite Order continue to pray for the people of the world.

The Carmelites continue to pray for all our pilgrims. Devotion to Saint Jude reminds us that God has the last word and Saint Jude reminds us that in times of darkness, God is there to lead us to the light that is God.

We remember all those who have asked for our prayers, those who bring hope and comfort during these difficult and painful times. The NHS and all key workers (Pandemic Heroes!) are very much in our thoughts and prayers. I know many of you have been personally affected by the virus through sickness and the sad death of loved ones, but also many of you have not seen friends and family for so long.

Let us pray...

Oh ever immaculate Virgin, Mother of Mercy, Health of the Sick, Refuge of Sinners, Comfortess of the Afflicted, you know my wants, my troubles, my sufferings. Look upon me with mercy. Amen.

Reflection was first published online on 5 February 2021

THOSE WHO SERVE US AT CHECKOUT

Fr Tim Finigan

Jamila was cross. She is not normally cheerful at the till, but now she was frustrated and angry at the elderly lady who had shouted at her, falsely accusing her of taking her basket away. I tried to distract Jamila because the elderly lady had dementia and was confused. It was the last hour of a long shift, the mask was uncomfortable, and the chair never seemed to position itself properly. She was not happy at her job anyway because she found too many customers inconsiderate and rude. Her husband had made it clear that he did not like her working in the supermarket because of the risk of Covid, but she knew they find it difficult to manage without the extra wages. The clerical collar can help to let people know that you are probably not going to be another customer who is impatient with the delay and might actually care just a little bit. God help us if we fail to achieve that minimal standard of charity.

On my way out, I called a quick "God bless" to Chioma at one of the other checkouts. Her loud laugh probably manages to intimidate at least some of the more grumpy shoppers and I guess that she refuses to let the daily nonsense get under her skin. When I get to use her till, we manage to swap quotations from the psalms; it helps that the King James Bible and the Douai Rheims are similar in style. In Lewisham, this kind of biblical banter is pleasantly frequent.

Some people love their job, others make the best of it, some endure it. The lockdown has taught us how much we rely on others, how much we really are members of society. We still say that people in shops "*serve*" us. That should remind us to be careful how we treat them, since they show to us the face of Jesus who said, "*I am in the midst of you, as he that serves.*"

Let us pray...

Blessed are You, Lord our God, Ruler of the universe, who creates the food that we eat. We pray for those who serve us. In your bountiful goodness, protect and strengthen them, their families and all who depend on them. Through Christ our Lord. Amen.

Reflection was first published online on 14 May 2021

WASTE COLLECTORS

Ms Trish Murphy

My next-door neighbour and I have an unspoken arrangement that she puts the bins out the day before they are due and I bring them back after the Waste Collectors have emptied them. Other neighbours remark that our bins being put out early lets them know which colour bin is due each week... Again there is something unspoken that has an importance in the smooth running of our lives.

I wonder if our appreciation of Waste Collectors is unspoken and what the workers might want us to say to them. Since the Covid Pandemic when I am bringing in the emptied bins, I often have a chance to greet the Waste Collectors and to say 'thank you'. But it is such a rush as they scurry along in their rhythmic team work that one might fear interfering with the pace of their work. However, there is always an acknowledgement and a brief connection. One suggested that I wear gloves 'because we touch so many different bins'. It is at times like this that I become aware of the pungent smell of waste and how our Collectors cannot escape this on every shift they work.

As a driver I am aware of my impatience if I am caught behind the Waste Collectors' vehicles and sometimes it takes a while to get past – revving the engine or constant looking at the clock is not going to help one bit. It's a God- given pause to reflect on what is happening and to be thankful... and in the end to be able to give a smile and friendly wave as the wait ends.

Where would we be without our Waste Collectors? They keep our environment healthy and safe especially in these times of heightened awareness of germs and viruses. They carry out their tasks in all types of weather. They know our seasons of waste: Christmas trees and wrappings; garden waste; summer partying waste; Halloween rubbish. Our Waste Collectors carry their own anxieties perhaps about their own wellness, about their work or about the health of their own loved ones...

Let us pray...

Listening and patient God we give thanks for our Waste Collectors. We ask you to protect them and their loved ones at all times and to bless them especially during times of difficulty. Help us to be mindful of our waste and above all let us not waste opportunities to say 'thank you' for all your daily gifts. Amen.

Reflection was first published online on 26 February 2021

NOT FORGETTING..

Those listed above are, of course, just a few of the Pandemic Heroes that have helped their fellow humans throughout this period, here are a few more* - each one brings light to this dark pandemic...

Mechanic
Deacon
Taxi Driver
Pharmacist
Dentist
Nursery worker
Firefighter
Security Guard
Porter
Priest
Plumber
Teaching Assistant
Zoo Keeper
Optician
Bus Driver
Vet
Sewage Engineer
Police Officer
Health Care Assistant
Prison Officer
Guard

* list not exhaustive! We pray and thank God for all the many Pandemic Heroes and for their service to us around the world.

Life, the Universe and Everything

The word of God is something alive and active
~ Hebrews 4:12

SAINT JOSEPH

Fr Gerard Walsh, O.Carm

Every Lent, we suspend the penitential season on the 19 March to celebrate the Solemnity Feast of Saint Joseph, the Husband of the Virgin Mary and for us Carmelites, the Principal Protector of the Carmelite Order. This year is an even bigger reason for celebrating, as we are in the Year of Saint Joseph, declared by Pope Francis last December. This coincides with the 150th Anniversary of Saint Joseph being declared the Patron of the Universal Church by Pope Pius IX in 1870.

All of us are familiar with Saint Joseph, the Foster-Father of Jesus, a man that appears in the New Testament and never says a word but by his actions we can really get to know him. I have always had a great devotion to Saint Joseph, having been brought up in a parish and going to a primary school that bears his name. I find in him a strong character and a saint we can always ask to intercede for us in all our needs. One of the episodes in Saint Joseph's life which has led to a popular devotion and has really touched me over the last number of years, is the devotion to the Sleeping Saint Joseph.

It was shortly after the election of Pope Francis that I became aware of this devotion. The Pope has a statue of Sleeping Joseph in his study and whenever he has a prayer intention that needs God's intervention, he writes it on a note and puts it under the Sleeping Joseph for him to dream about it. For a while now I have been doing the same. It helps me to manage my own prayer requests, and also I know they are safe under the gaze of such a powerful intercessor.

During this Year of Saint Joseph, I have observed that this devotion is increasing in popularity, precisely because it is a practical prayer suggestion that speaks to people's hearts. So, we invite you to ask Saint Joseph, our Spiritual Father, to intercede for all your needs, especially during these trying times and as he protected Jesus and Mary in their vulnerability, allow him to protect you.

Let us pray...

O Saint Joseph, you are a man greatly favoured by the Most High. The angel of the Lord appeared to you in dreams, while you slept, to warn you and guide you as you cared for the Holy Family. You were both silent and strong, a loyal and courageous protector. Dear Saint Joseph, as you rest in the Lord, confident of his absolute power and goodness, look upon me. Please take my need into your heart, dream of it, and present it to your son. Help me then, good Saint Joseph, to hear the voice of God, to arise, and to act with love. I praise and thank God with joy. Saint Joseph, I love you. Amen.

Reflection was first published online on 19 March 2021

GOD, IN WHOM I TRUST

Mr Aldrick Monteiro

Do you wish you could win the Lottery,
Is advanced aging causing you grief?
Are you wanting, struggling and feeling doddery,
Have you no self worth or belief?

How many times have you felt hopeless,
Contemplating how futile life can be?
When were you last blessed with real happiness?
When did you last open your eyes to see?

God is all-knowing and all-seeing,
He knows your life and your fate.
God is in the very depths of your being,
Access him now before it is too late.

He promises a full life to all who believe,
Asking us to love our neighbour, and forgive.
His requests are not impossible to achieve,
With God's guidance, we can truly live.

Christ came to earth without his glory,
He came that men might find their God.
He came with a wonderful blessed story,
Of salvation and hope from Our Lord.

It would not be easy he candidly had said,
He would not take away every ill and pain.
If we persevered, we would be rewarded,
In Heaven with Jesus, we would reign.

Jesus died for all, once and for ever,
The salvific business was done on Calvary.
The devil was defeated, and now would never,
Be the cause of endless adversity.

Reflection was first published online on 28 May 2021

HOLINESS

Mr John Hartley

"Do everything without complaining or arguing so that you may be innocent and pure" - Phil. 2 14-15

Many years ago, I read a book by Donald Nicholl entitled "Holiness". The book adopted a lay-oriented practical approach to its subject. One of its exhortations was "Do not complain!" In our western democracies we have become spoilt by the freedoms we enjoy. We all revel in criticising authority, while the press enjoys enormous power in its ability to stir up our critical nature. The Covid crisis has engendered some good and much-needed debate about what government policy should be. But it has also magnified our resentments when freedoms to which we believe we have an absolute right are taken away. And so we mutter and complain with what we believe is righteous anger – failing to understand that saving lives is paramount, and that the government has an unenviable task on its hands.

Admittedly, without public protest many great wrongs would not have been righted. Slavery would not have been abolished, nor would the exploitation of child labour. The Black Lives Matter movement would not have got underway; and our National Health Service would not have come into existence. But this reflection is about our personal attitude towards things with which we disagree, not about the need for social or political movements.

My brother, who was a Cistercian monk for 56 years before he died in 2010, would always attempt to recall the words of Psalm 15/16 when he was upset or disappointed about the way things were being done in the monastery, or frustrated by an unwelcome task he had been given:

"Welcome indeed the heritage that falls to me
The lot marked out for me is my delight"

Those words are a precept of acceptance and obedience. They are ones that we westerners find alien to the independence and freedom of action we claim to be our birth right.

My son Christopher, who works in the hotel industry, told me once how important it is to complain about poor service or poor food. *'How else can improvement be achieved?'* he asked. In the business world his advice is certainly correct. But in the other world in which we are aspiring to holiness, must not an uncomplaining spirit of acceptance and obedience be our aim?

Let us pray...

Breathe in me, O Holy Spirit, that my thoughts may all be holy.
Act in me, O Holy Spirit, that my work, too, may be holy.
Draw my heart, O Holy Spirit, that I love only what is holy.
Strengthen me, O Holy Spirit, to defend all that is holy.
Guard me so, O Holy Spirit, that I may always be holy.
Amen.

Reflection was first published online on 26 March 2021

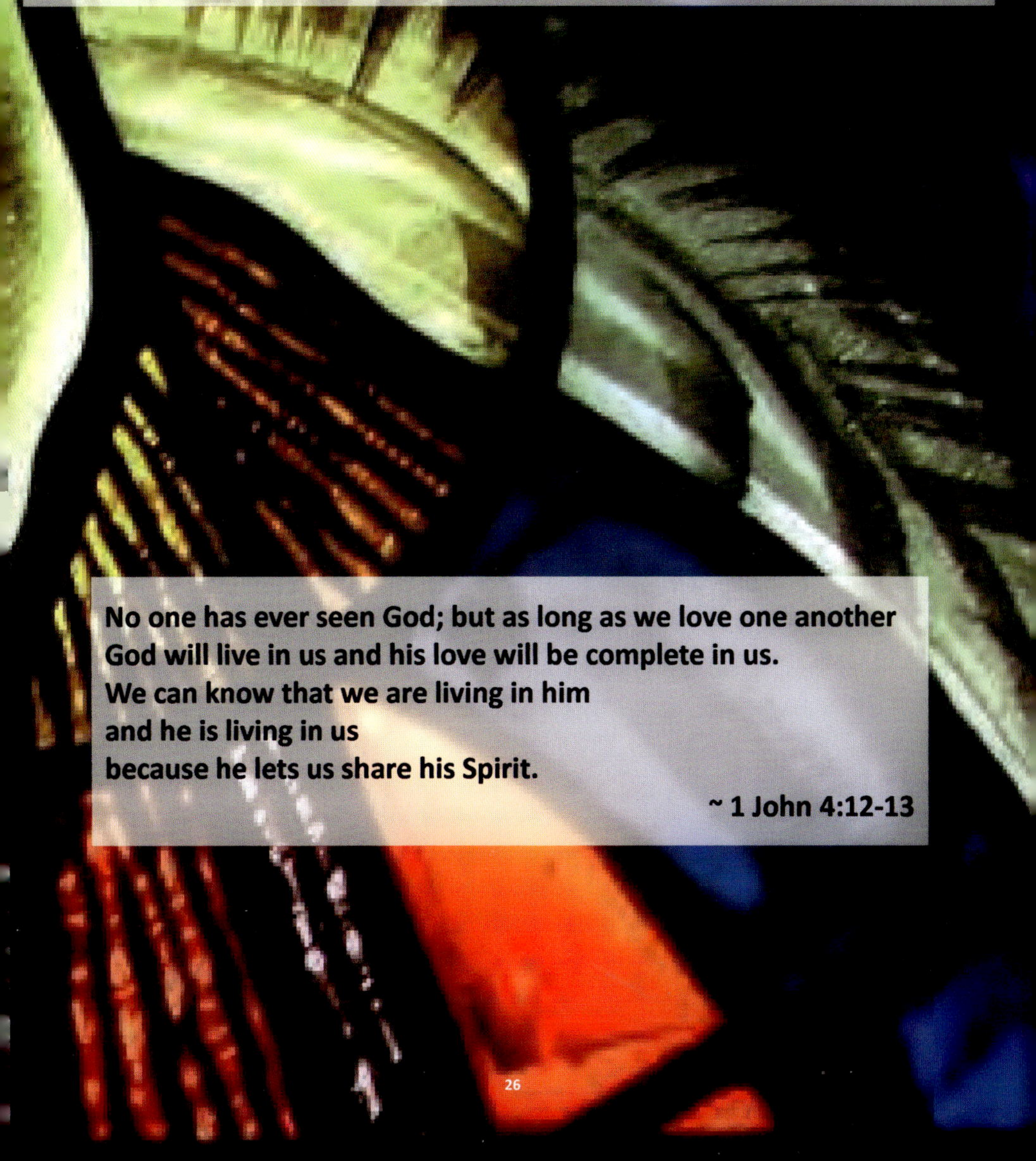

No one has ever seen God; but as long as we love one another
God will live in us and his love will be complete in us.
We can know that we are living in him
and he is living in us
because he lets us share his Spirit.

~ 1 John 4:12-13

FOUR PEOPLE YOU MEET IN LIFE

Mr Matthew Betts

A while back, I read the book 'The Five People You Meet in Heaven'. I am sure that some of you have read it too, but if you haven't, here is a brief introduction: the book tells the story of Eddie, an 83-year-old amusement park maintenance worker who is killed while trying to save a child from being crushed by a malfunctioning ride. Eddie finds himself in heaven, where he is told that he will begin his eternal journey by meeting the five people who had the most profound influence on his life.

My reflections are not about the novel per se, i.e. meeting people in heaven, but instead I want you to join me in a journey by thinking about four people (I've not got room for five, but maybe I'll do a sequel) that you have met in your life and who have influenced you in a good way. I will discuss four people I have met and although I have changed one or two names, these people exist.

- Think about four people you have met in your life and who have had an influence on your life - however small the meeting. How have they helped? Can you thank God for them?

The first person I want to mention is a lady called Hilda. I was seventeen and going to Our Lady's Shrine in Lourdes for the first time as a volunteer helper. Lourdes is truly a beautiful place and, I believe, it is the only place in the whole world where sick people are put FIRST. This is where I met Hilda.

She was an 80-something lady who wanted to go shopping to get religious gifts for her grandchildren. I was so nervous and kept pushing her wheelchair into the drains outside the shops. She told me not to worry as she was having a great time. However, I was devastated – this poor woman trusted me and I had been a terrible pusher!

The next day, she was laughing with the other ladies in her ward, telling them all about this young chap (me!) who had been so funny, charming and caring. She explained later that I had kept her laughing during our trip with all the shenanigans, and she hadn't had so much fun for ages. She also told me that I had shown her care and concern throughout and never let her down. I enjoyed taking Hilda out shopping many more times after (but with less drains!) Sometimes people see something different from what you see!

- Have you ever been surprised by someone who doesn't see the bad – just the good? Can you be more like that?

In the South East, there's a parish that I used to go to a number of times a year. We would run charity events in their parish hall, and we met a number of people who had lived in the parish for many years, and in some cases, all of their lives. The following saying comes from Jesus and sums up the parishioners – they were all the salt of the earth. It was a tough area to live in as a lot of the community spirit was being eroded, but even so, each person was full of joy and happiness.

I am going to mention two people that my wife and I met: Paula and Rob. They worked behind the bar and were the kindest, loveliest people. Very quickly, my wife and I realised we shared a very similar sense of humour to them, and so every time we met up, we would laugh a lot. Sometimes, I think, God provides chances to meet people like Paula and Rob to remind us that love is everywhere. We enjoyed their company so much, we invited them to our wedding – and they came. We laughed lots that day too. I will always be grateful that we met them.

- Have you met someone who has made you smile each time you see them? Can you find happiness in what you are doing each day? Why not thank God for every moment that has made you smile?

The fourth person I would like to mention, is my step-grandfather, Edward. He married my Nan (grandmother) seven years before I was born.

Looking back, Edward was the real version of an archetypal character from a PG Wodehouse book (if you've not read Wodehouse, please do). Anyway, Edward was a little bit eccentric, but full of fascinating facts, thoughts and sayings. One of his favourite sayings was "*take an orange out of the box*", which was said for when we had done well! So, now I try and reward good behaviour from my children with a healthy snack! Brilliant.

Although as a boy, I found his sayings and thoughts a little bit old-fashioned, in later life, I've actually found myself taking them on-board. One of the best pieces of advice he gave me was to always try and find the good in everything and everyone, however bad things might seem.

As we know, Saint Jude went out and told the Good News of Jesus Christ. He later became the patron saint of "desperate" or "difficult" cases (a term used in preference to the older title of "hopeless", since with God no situation is hopeless). Jude is thus a saint of hope. Let's pray to Saint Jude that we may find good - and thus hope - in all things.

- Why not speak to Jude and thank him for spreading the Good News? Can you do some good for someone today?

Reflection was first published online on 21 August 2021

MARY AND EASTER

Fr Kevin Alban, O.Carm

The presence of Mary in the gospel accounts is highly significant, but suddenly after the Crucifixion she seems to disappear, only to re-emerge very briefly in the Acts of the Apostles in the upper room, praying with the disciples as they await the Holy Spirit. Outside the scriptures, other writers have asserted strongly that the Risen Lord appears to his mother. Saint Ambrose, the fourth-century bishop of Milan, states: "*Mary saw the Lord's resurrection. She was the first who saw and believed.*" In the Spiritual Exercises of Saint Ignatius of Loyola, founder of the Jesuits, the Fourth week begins with a meditation on the appearance of the Risen Christ to Mary. Surely it would have been impossible for the Risen Lord not to have appeared to his mother? Yet the gospels do not record this. There are some complex reasons behind this, but perhaps there is also something to help us as well.

Mary's attitude in the gospels of Luke and John is particularly instructive here. In Luke we see a woman who is trying to make sense of the reality that she encounters:

- But Mary was very confused about what the angel said. She wondered, "*What does this mean?*" - Luke 1:29
- Everyone was surprised when they heard what the shepherds told them. Mary continued to think about these things, trying to understand them. - Luke 2:18-19
- But they did not understand the meaning of what he said to them. Jesus went with them to Nazareth and obeyed them. His mother was still thinking about all these things. - Luke 2: 50-51

The meaning of the phrase "*thinking about these things*" is that Mary was trying to work out what was happening to her. She is faced with some confusing and strange scenarios and she wants to understand what is happening and how she fits in. She does not claim to have all the answers, but she is prepared to think about and make sense of the reality around her. We are faced with the reality of the Church's preaching that Christ has risen. How do we understand this in our own lives and what does it mean for the way we see our place in the Church's preaching?

If we fast forward from the accounts of Jesus' birth and infancy to his Crucifixion, then we see a group of women in Luke's gospel who watch the Crucifixion. Was Mary in this group? Or was she devastated by what was happening to her son? Both reactions are possible, both are normal, both are human. Do we have the courage to contemplate the Crucifixion or do we turn away, unable to bear it? Mary helps us in either case – a woman of courage, but also a mother.

Whatever we make of Mary's presence or not at the Crucifixion, she was certainly with the disciples in the upper room: "The apostles were all together. They were constantly praying with the same purpose. Some women, Mary the mother of Jesus, and his brothers were there with the apostles." - Acts 1:14

It is fairly clear that Mary has come to believe in the resurrection of her son, drawing on her capacity to work out the meaning and truth of the reality she encounters. She is also able to translate that discovery into engagement with the early Church – that same group of men and women she had known during her son's ministry, but now transformed by faith. This challenges us to not only believe, but to put that belief into practice in prayer and in community. Presumably she shared not only the spiritual life of the group, but also the lifestyle that we read about:

"All the believers stayed together and shared everything. They sold their land and the things they owned. Then they divided the money and gave it to those who needed it". - Acts 2: 44-45

Our belief in the resurrection changes the way we live and interact with each other and with the world – and Mary is part of this process.

On Good Friday in the account of the Passion we read from Saint John's Gospel the poignant and iconic incident of the Mother of Jesus at the Foot of the Cross.

"Jesus' mother stood near his cross. Her sister was also standing there with Mary the wife of Clopas, and Mary Magdalene. Jesus saw his mother. He also saw the follower he loved very much standing there. He said to his mother, "Dear woman, here is your son." Then he said to the follower, "Here is your mother." So after that, this follower took Jesus' mother to live in his home." - John 19: 25-27

This scene has given rise to production in the visual arts and in music, so moving and profound an image does it present. However, to appreciate it fully, we must connect it with the only other appearance of the Mother of Jesus in John's gospel at the Wedding Feast at Cana. In that scene Jesus' mother encourages him to begin his ministry and show his concern for the young couple who are about to see their banquet ruined.

This scene is, however, more than a lesson in how to cope with embarrassing social occasions. The key words are when Mary turns to the waiters and says. "*Do whatever he tells you.*" They are words that echo the fundamental relationship of the people of Israel and God himself – the obedience implied in the covenant that Moses announces.

At the foot of the Cross, Mary witnesses the climax of her son's ministry and his concern now is for her directly. No longer does Jesus give his instructions to the waiters, but now he instructs the Beloved Disciple and his own mother. She must exercise her maternal role over the new community, symbolised by that disciple. He in turn must treat her as a mother with the same care and concern that Jesus showed. Both commands are quite challenging. Mary arrives at the scene of Jesus' Crucifixion accompanied by her sister, Mary the wife of Clopas and Mary Magdalene.

She must now move from the role she has with her relatives and friends to a new role at the heart of the praying Church, as Luke describes it. In the midst of the horror and grief of the Crucifixion how does she react? What are her feelings and reactions? One of the most striking aspects of this scene is her silence. At Cana she spoke, she asked, she told the waiters to listen to her son. Now she is silently faced with her dying son who now instructs her. But her silence is a fertile one. She clearly takes her son's words to heart and obeys his command.

There are many ways we can draw on the figure of Mary and her role in the Easter season and I would suggest that she helps us move from a passive role in the Resurrection. We do contemplate the mystery of the Risen Lord and that is an important part of our prayer life. At the same time, Mary reminds us that the Resurrection challenges us in a number of ways. It tests the way we think about this mystery in our lives. It makes us think about our role in the Church. It asks us to change our lives. And Mary can be a model for all these demands.

Let us pray...

Hail Mary, full of grace,
the Lord is with thee.
Blessed art thou amongst women,
and blessed is the fruit of thy womb, Jesus.
Holy Mary, Mother of God,
pray for us sinners,
now and at the hour of our death. Amen.

Reflection was first published online on 27 April 2020

SAINT JUDE AND FRIENDSHIP

Dr Johan Bergström-Allen, TOC

So many people speak affectionately about Saint Jude being their "friend". Pilgrims often refer to "our friend Saint Jude" when they come to the Apostle's National Shrine in Faversham. Devotees get in touch with us Carmelites via the Shrine Office and social media, asking for the prayers of Jude Thaddeus "our faithful friend". The newsletter that the Carmelites distribute from the National Shrine is likewise addressed to "Dear Friends of Saint Jude", and through the Guild of Saint Jude I feel part of a network of friends.

One definition of friends is "the family we choose for ourselves". A friend is someone we feel especially close to, someone we trust. Everyone has passing acquaintances, but friendship is a much stronger bond. We bond to friends with ties of mutual affection. We can share our hopes and dreams with a friend, as well as our problems and worries. Friends are people we can be intimate with, speaking informally and honestly. When I talk to Saint Jude in prayer, I like to speak to him as a friend:

Saint Jude, friend of God and friend of mine, thank you for your love and care for me, and for those I hold dear. Help me, today, to be a true friend to those I encounter. Like you, I want to be a reflection of God's love in the world. Saint Jude, my friend, pray for us.

Friends with God

The Carmelite friars are brothers in a contemplative religious order. One simple definition of 'contemplation' is 'being friends with God'. God already loves us, and we don't have to convince God to do so, because love is God's very nature. All we have to do in the relationship is to turn to God with open hearts, and accept God's free gift of friendship.

If we are unsure how to do that – how to deepen our friendship with God – a great way to learn is to follow the examples of Saint Jude and his fellow apostles, those who first followed in the footsteps of Jesus and became intimate with him. In the Gospel accounts we get wonderful glimpses of the warm friendship that existed, and still exists, between Jesus and those who lived alongside him in Palestine 2000 years ago:

Almighty God, you sent your Son Jesus into the world to share the Good News of how much you love us. No one is separated from your free offer of friendship. I offer you today my open heart to love as you do, my open mind to know your will, and my open hands to serve those around me, especially the most poor and needy. Amen. Saint Jude, our friend, pray for us.

Friends with our neighbours

As an apostle, one of Jesus's most devoted followers, Saint Jude was no doubt present when Our Lord said that the greatest commandments are to "*love the Lord your God with all your heart*", and to "*love your neighbour as yourself*". When a lawyer asked Jesus "*Who is my neighbour?*", Our Lord replied by telling him the parable of the Good Samaritan who helped a traveller who had been robbed and beaten half to death.

The neighbour in that story was not the priest who passed by on the other side, or the Levite (who assisted at religious rites in the Temple). It was the Samaritan – from a group of people looked down on by Jesus's own contemporaries – who "showed mercy". Jesus teaches us that our religious observances are worthless if we fail to show mercy to those in need, and friendship can come from the most unexpected people.

Lord Jesus, best of friends, may my faith not lead me to think that I am better than other people, or prevent me from helping others in messy situations. When I see my neighbour in need, whoever and wherever that might be, give me a merciful heart full of friendship, ready to bring your healing touch and word of hope. Amen. Saint Jude, friend of all, pray for us.

Friends with ourselves

Jesus said that we should love God, and "*your neighbour as yourself*". The psychologist Carl Jung said that the problem with the world is precisely that we don't love ourselves, and so we don't love our neighbours. We shouldn't be proud, vain, or selfish, but we should have a proper and healthy love for ourselves. God loves us with an infinite love, and who are we to say that God has got it wrong?! We are made in God's image, and enjoy the dignity of the children of God. Yes, we are all sinners, but we are loved and forgiven sinners. Jesus gave everything – even his own life – to show us that there is nothing God will not give us. Nothing can separate us from the love and friendship of God.

Tender-hearted God, friend of friends, it is often so easy for me to be hard on myself. Instead of hearing you say, "You are my child, I love you", I pay attention to that nagging voice which says, "You're worthless, no one loves you." But I know, deep down in my heart, that you DO love me, and that I am precious in your sight. Help me to have a healthy love of myself, from which I will be better able to love those around me. Through Jesus Christ our Lord and friend. Amen. Saint Jude, my friend, pray for me.

When friendships hurt

Wonderful as friendship is, there are times when we hurt others, or are let down by others, even the closest of friends. At these moments it can be hard to forgive ourselves, or other people. Even Saint Jude and his fellow apostles failed to be a friend to Jesus when Our Lord was arrested and put on trial. Yet Jesus never closed the door on friendship, never reproached his disciples for their lack of faith. Instead, when Jesus ascended to his Father and ours, he promised to send the Holy Spirit to be our advocate, to plead our cause as a friend.

Holy Spirit of God, you are present wherever there is friendship and love. Help me to grow in friendship with you, with others, and with myself. Heal those relationships where friendship and trust have broken down. Help me to forgive those who have hurt me, and to extend the hand of friendship to those I find it hard to get on with. Speak, act, and love in me and through me. Amen. Saint Jude, friend of sinners, pray for me.

Friendship in Carmel

The Carmelites established the National Shrine of Saint Jude because many friends of the Order wrote to Faversham asking for prayer cards of the Apostle. The Shrine founder, Father Elias Lynch, recognised that many people saw Saint Jude as their friend, especially in difficult and desperate situations.

As a Carmelite, Father Elias was rooted in a spirituality that deeply treasures the idea of friendship. Many Carmelite saints have spoken of their relationship with God, and with others, in terms of friendship. Saint Teresa of Avila called Jesus her "closest friend", and wrote to her fellow Carmelite nuns that "all must be friends with each other, love each other, be fond of each other, and help each other". Saint Thérèse of Lisieux described God as a friend she could have complete confidence in.

God our Father and our friend, we thank you for the friendship we have in the communion of saints. The Apostles, the Saints of Carmel, and all your holy people are friends whose intercession and example we can trust in. May your love shine out through the Carmelites, and through the whole Church, so that all may be drawn to friendship with you. Amen. Saint Jude, model of friendship, pray for us.

Friendship with strangers

One of the mysteries of friendship is how love can bind people together, even when they've never met. Friends of Saint Jude support the Carmelites through their donations and their prayers, and this benefits the Order not only in Britain but throughout the world.

There are countless people and projects in some of the most financially-deprived parts of our world who have experienced the friendship of God through the material and spiritual support of Saint Jude's friends. In his encyclical, Fratelli Tutti (Brothers and Sisters All) Pope Francis reminds us that Christians must nurture a sense of fraternity and solidarity with everyone. For the Christian no one is really a stranger, just a friend who has yet to be met.

Lord Jesus, you teach us the true meaning of friendship. Help us to welcome strangers as friends, and to know that the whole world is connected by our common humanity. May a spirit of friendship overcome all attitudes that marginalise people because of their colour, religion, ideas, gender, race, education, culture, ability, or identity. You have reached out in friendship to us; may we respond generously by reaching out to others, especially those who suffer from poverty, discrimination, sickness, or neglect. Amen. Saint Jude, friend to one and all, pray for us.

Reflection was first published online on 4 and 11 June 2021

May mercy, peace, and love be yours in abundance...To the only God our Saviour, through Jesus Christ our Lord, be glory, majesty, power, and authority, before all time and now and for ever. Amen.

~ Letter of Saint Jude

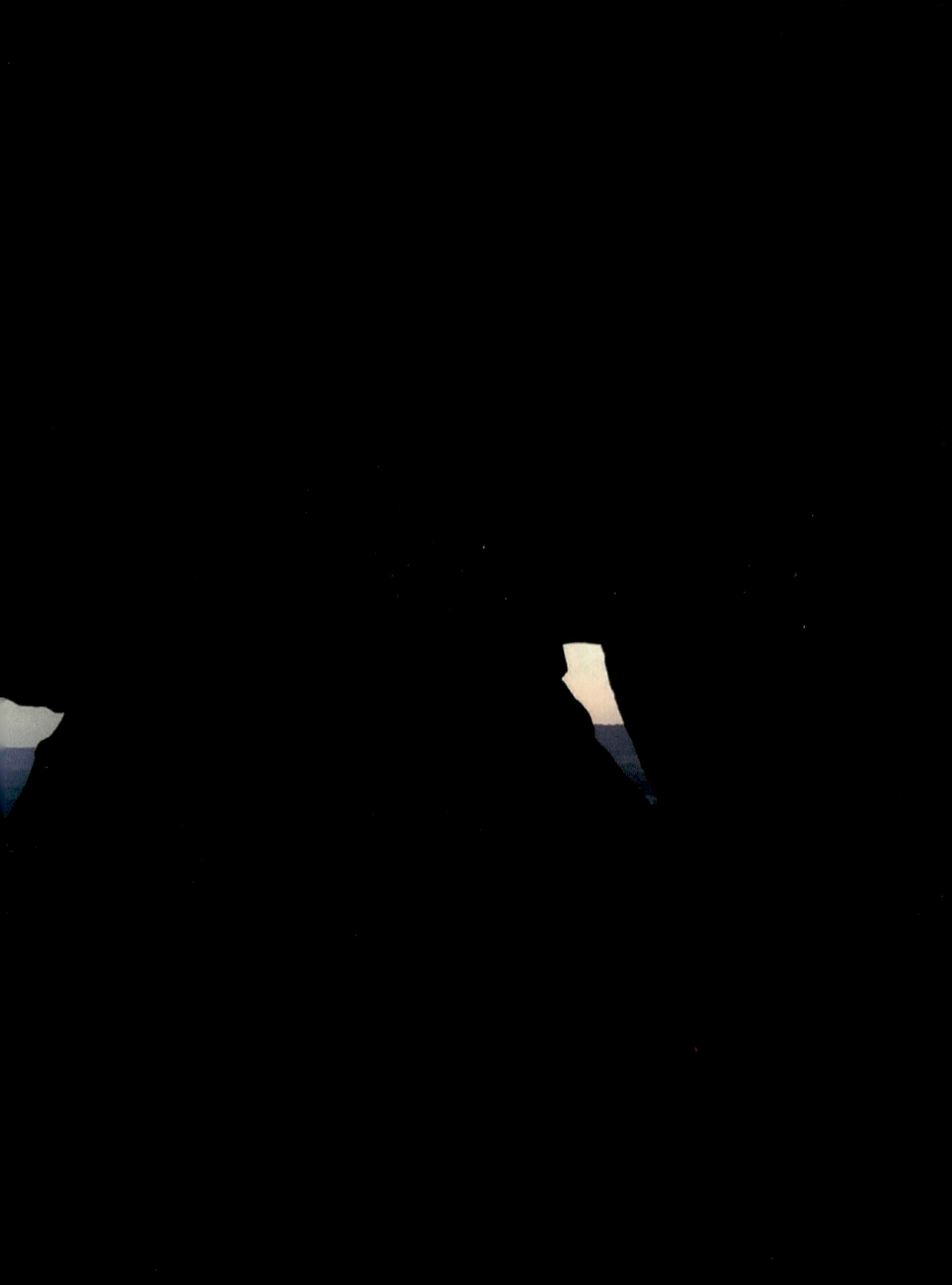

In Appreciation
I give them eternal life, and they shall never perish...
~ John 10:28-30

AN APPRECIATION OF VERY REV. PROFESSOR KEVIN ALBAN, O.CARM

Professor Peter Tyler

I first met Father Kevin over a long lunch in Rome, which may come as no surprise to many of you here. At the time we were both working at the Beda College in the Eternal City, the validation for whose degrees had just recently been taken over by my university, St Mary's, Twickenham. I was the moderator of the degree and Father Kevin was one of the examiners. We spent most of the meal discussing the merits of various Roman cheeses and by the end had decided to organise an international conference to celebrate the 500th anniversary of the birth of Saint Teresa of Avila - which eventually took place with great success in 2015.

I think this initial encounter set the tone for our collaboration and friendship: a wonderful combination of conviviality, practical projects and spiritual wisdom. One of my friends tells me that when she was discerning a religious vocation he advised her 'God will never be outdone with generosity'. And that was really his watchword – 'generosity'. Since his death I have had many conversations with students and colleagues alike, who have told me little stories about the extra generosity he showed as a teacher, mentor and friend. This was my own experience too. Whenever I asked him to do something - he did it and then added a little extra. It was that 'more' which students responded to and loved about him. He had a great mind, a great heart and a great capacity for life.

Last week we had a doctoral supervision with a student he had been advising and I asked the question whether we ought to replace Father Kevin on the team. As we discussed it we realised - he was irreplaceable. His knowledge of late medieval religious culture and his Latin scholarship was unrivalled – even though he did usually conclude that the answer to most late medieval theological questions could be summed up in two words: 'Thomas Netter'. I am sure he is enjoying catching up with the doctor authenticus, his fellow Prior Provincial, on some celestial cloud even as we speak.

This love and enthusiasm for medieval Carmelite spirituality made him a leading expert in the field and over the years he contributed much to the establishment of St Mary's MA in Christian Spirituality. In the last conversation we had a few weeks ago we were discussing how he could contribute to our new doctoral programmes.

In fact, over the ten years in which we knew each other I can only remember one occasion when we had a cross word. That was the time when we co-led a pilgrimage to Spain, another of his great loves, and I gave a lecture on Saint John of the Cross, referring to John's 'imprisonment' in Toledo by the Carmelites.

"Imprisonment", Father Kevin chuckled, "a very harsh word Peter" – "John had become radicalised – it was a de-radicalisation programme he was participating in..."

As we sit now in the Church's calendar between Ascension and Pentecost, I think Father Kevin would approve if I ended with the final lines of the medieval Latin hymn to the Holy Spirit, Veni Sancte Spiritus, as we commend his soul to the Lord's mercy and thank God for the life of this wise, witty and wonderful man, the Very Rev. Professor Kevin Alban O.Carm:

Da virtutis meritum
Da salutis exitum
Da perenne gaudium

Grant, Lord, the reward of virtue
Grant salvation at the end
Grant him everlasting joy

Amen

AFTERWORD

Archbishop John Wilson

It was just over two weeks or so between my final visit to Father Kevin Alban before his death at Aylesford Priory, surrounded by his community, in the home he loved. We spoke about the gift of faith. How it can be challenged by suffering, but, for a disciple, never totally erased. For those of us who follow the Lord Jesus, even pain and loss, illness, and death, carry the hue of the resurrection. Father Kevin reflected that, even though his own situation had now changed, the Lord remained the same. He gave powerful witness to Christ, as a believer, a friar, and a priest. Before I left, we exchanged blessings, mutual gifts of love and hope, united prayerfully in the Lord.

It sounds trite to say the pandemic has changed our world and lives. For some people, the impact has been devastating, with loss of life, leaving loved ones behind, sometimes without the chance to say a proper goodbye or to grieve at a funeral surrounded by family and friends. For others, relationships have been strained, loneliness has become more pronounced, and even day to day existence has been a burden. When so much has changed, how important it is to focus on what remains the same. This is true too as we step out into a new future. For Christians this means remembering the Lord is indeed risen. Without this truth at the centre of our lives then, not only is our faith in vain, but our hope is reduced merely to the tensions, tragedies, and limitations of this present world.

So many people have shared with me the importance of their faith during the pandemic, even when our churches were closed, and it was not possible to attend Mass in person. When we were allowed to open our churches for private prayer, a lady wrote to say the first time she was able to visit the Blessed Sacrament again she simply sat and wept.

Whatever is happening in our lives, or the lives of those around us, whatever is happening in our world, we remain people of faith in Christ. He is with us. This is the unshakable faith of a disciple. Whatever happens, I am not alone. Whatever happens, even the worst thing imaginable, Christ is with us, he who trampled sin and death and rose victorious from the grave.

From the anguish and pain of the pandemic we have witnessed an overflow of self-giving, from key workers and unsung heroes and heroines, between neighbours and total strangers, with churches playing their part. What can we learn from the pandemic? Apart from making sure we appreciate fully the people and things that matter most, perhaps we can hear anew the call for each one of us to be a blessing to others. How that blessing happens will depend on the circumstances. But might we choose to bless those we meet, whoever they are?

Can we bless them with kindness, generosity, and compassion? Can we see Christ in them and let them see Christ in us?

+ John

Yes, I am sure that nothing can separate us from God's love—not death, life, angels, or ruling spirits. I am sure that nothing now, nothing in the future, no powers, nothing above us or nothing below us—nothing in the whole created world—will ever be able to separate us from the love God has shown us in Christ Jesus our Lord.

~ Romans 8:38-39

INDEX OF PHOTOGRAPHS

INDEX OF PHOTOGRAPHS

A prayer for those with COVID-19

Dear Lord,
in your ministry, you healed and cared for everyone regardless of age, sex, creed or position in society.

Be with all the people who need you because of COVID-19. Protect those who will feel isolated whilst they are in quarantine or whilst receiving treatment.

Help all those who look after the sick. Give them strength for this selfless service, enabling them to give hope to those they are called to serve.

Help people to work together rather than individually, just as Jesus did with his Apostles.

Saint Jude, saint of hope, pray for us.

Amen.

Prayer written by Matthew Betts

My Lord God

My Lord God,
I have no idea where I am going.
I do not see the road ahead of me.
I cannot know for certain where it will end
nor do I really know myself,
and the fact that I think I am following your will
does not mean that I am actually doing so.
But I believe that the desire to please you
does in fact please you.
And I hope I have that desire in all that I am doing.
I hope that I will never do anything apart from that desire.
And I know that if I do this you will lead me by the right road,
though I may know nothing about it.
Therefore will I trust you always though
I may seem to be lost and in the shadow of death.
I will not fear, for you are ever with me,
and you will never leave me to face my perils alone.

~ Thomas Merton, 1915 - 1968

ALSO AVAILABLE

God in the Time of COVID-19 - Book One

Saint Jude Prayer Book

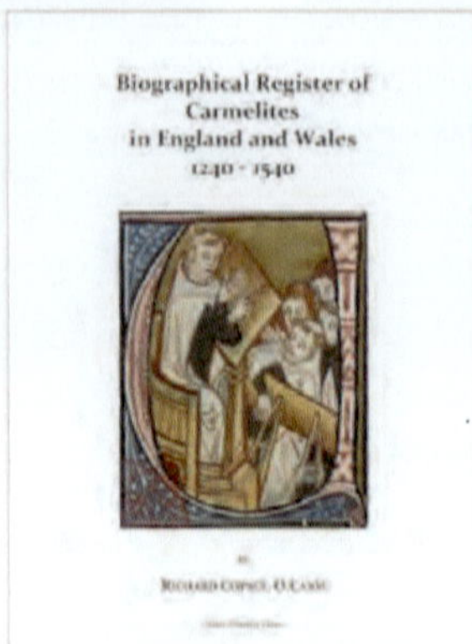

Biographical Register of Carmelites in England and Wales: 1240 - 1540

These and other titles can be ordered from:

https://stjudeshrine.co.uk/

The Shrine of Saint Jude
Carmelite Friars
PO Box 289
Faversham
Kent
ME13 3BZ

Tel: 01795 539 214

The Friars Bookshop
The Friars
Aylesford
Kent
ME20 7BX

Tel: 01622 715 770